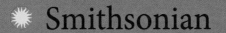

※ **Smithsonian**

LITTLE EXPLORER

Motion

by Megan Cooley Peterson

PEBBLE
a capstone imprint

Little Explorer is published by Pebble,
1710 Roe Crest Drive, North Mankato, Minnesota 56003
www.capstonepub.com

The name of the Smithsonian Institution and the sunburst logo are registered
trademarks of the Smithsonian Institution. For more information, please
visit www.si.edu.

Library of Congress Cataloging-in-Publication Data
Names: Peterson, Megan Cooley, author. Title: Motion / by Megan Cooley Peterson.
Description: North Mankato, Minnesota : Pebble, a Capstone imprint, [2020] | Series:
Smithsonian little explorer. Little physicist | Audience: 6–8. | Audience: K to Grade 3.
Identifiers: LCCN 2019005131 | ISBN 9781977109637 (hardcover) | ISBN 1977109632
(hardcover) | ISBN 9781977110664 (pbk.) | ISBN 1977110665 (pbk.) | ISBN
9781977109675 (eBook PDF) | ISBN 1977109675 (eBook PDF) Subjects:
LCSH: Motion—Juvenile literature. Classification: LCC QC133.5 .P48 2020 |
DDC 531/.11—dc23 LC record available at https://lccn.loc.gov/2019005131

Editorial Credits
Michelle Parkin, editor; Kyle Grenz, designer; Eric Gohl, media researcher;
Tori Abraham, production specialist

Our very special thanks to Henry D. Winter III, PhD, Astrophysicist, Center for
Astrophysics, Harvard and Smithsonian. Capstone would also like to thank
Kealy Gordon, Product Development Manager, and the following at Smithsonian
Enterprises: Ellen Nanney, Licensing Manager; Brigid Ferraro, Vice President, Education
and Consumer Products; and Carol LeBlanc, Senior Vice President, Education and
Consumer Products.

Image Credits
Alamy: Jim West, 8–9; iStockphoto: apomares, 1, Brian Nolan, 21, gbh007, 29, Miklmar,
5, People Images, 23 (top), xefstock, 13; Newscom: ZUMA Press/Jim Dedmon, 25;
Shutterstock: Alexandra Lande, 11, Anastacia Leskina, 15, cammep, 4 (hare), CyberKat,
4 (falcon), Evannovostro, background (throughout), Hennadii H, 4 (sailfish), Lawrence
Roberg, 24, Michael Deemer, 12, Monkey Business Images, 7 (top), Narong Khueankaew,
27, NCS Production, cover, Paradise On Earth, 17 (bottom), Pat Hastings, 14, Rostislav
Stefanek, 26, Sergey Ginak, 19 (inset), Skycolors, 18–19, supergenijalac, 20, timurockart,
23 (bottom), Vadim Sadovski, 10, VectorArtFactory, 4 (cheetah), Wanchai Orsuk, 17 (top);
SuperStock: Bridgeman Art Library, London, 7 (bottom)

All internet sites appearing in back matter were available and accurate when this book
was sent to press.

Printed in the United States of America.
PA70

Table of Contents

What Is Motion?

A roller coaster slowly moves up the track. It pauses at the top of the first hill. Then the car speeds down the track. *Whoosh!* Life would be boring without motion.

We use motion every day. We brush our teeth in the morning. We walk to the school bus stop. Your eyes are moving as you read this page. Life on Earth could not exist without motion.

The Fastest on Earth

What are the fastest animals on the planet?

brown hares	**sailfish**	**cheetahs**	**peregrine falcons**

run up to 48 miles (77 kilometers) per hour	swim as fast as 68 miles (109 km) per hour	run up to 70 miles (113 km) per hour	dive up to 200 miles (322 km) per hour

Let's Get Moving!

It's a school day. You're in class when you hear the lunch bell. *Ring!* You walk to your locker and grab your lunch. How did you walk down the hallway?

Motion needs forces. A force is a push or pull. Forces make objects change directions. They also make objects speed up or slow down. When you walked down the hall, your leg muscles made a force. This force pushed your body into motion.

> Your body is always in motion. Your heart beats. Blood flows. Your lungs breathe in and out.

The Three Laws of Motion

Scientist Isaac Newton studied motion in the mid-1600s. He used math to explain why objects move. His ideas became known as the Three Laws of Motion. They explain how motion works.

Law 1:
An object at rest will stay at rest until a force moves it. An object in motion needs a force to stop it.

Law 2:
An object's speed changes based on its mass and the forces acting on it.

Law 3:
Every force has an equal and opposite force.

Motion and Forces

Objects at rest won't move without a force. Imagine standing on ice in skates. You need your legs to push you forward. Without a push, you won't move.

Objects in motion won't stop without a force. Drop your pencil. What happens? It falls until the floor stops it.

A Newton is the standard international unit used to measure force.

Gravity

You can't see gravity. But this force is all around you. Gravity pulls objects toward the center of Earth. Without gravity, you would float into space!

Meteors are pieces of space rock caught in Earth's gravity.

Imagine you are sailing through the air in a hang glider. You can't stay up there forever. The glider will keep going until the force of gravity pulls it to the ground.

We're Shrinking!

Did you know that gravity causes us to shrink? During the day, gravity pulls down on our bodies. This pulling makes our spines squish together. When we lie down at night, our spines stretch out again.

Mass, Weight, and Motion

Mass is the amount of matter in an object. Objects with more mass need stronger forces to move them. A chair has more mass than a pencil. It takes a stronger force to lift the chair.

Weight is not the same as mass. Weight measures gravity's pull on an object.

Gravity keeps the oceans on Earth. The moon also has gravity. The moon's gravity pulls the ocean water toward it. This pulling causes ocean tides.

Gravity pulls harder on objects that have more mass.

The heavier object has more mass.

Magnets and Motion

Have you ever put a magnet onto a refrigerator? It sticks. A magnet can also move some metals without touching them.

A magnet pushes and pulls. It has an invisible magnetic force field. The magnet has two poles. They are called the north pole and south pole. A magnet's force field flows from its north to south pole.

Magnets stick to some metals, such as iron and steel. They don't stick to other metals, such as copper and aluminum.

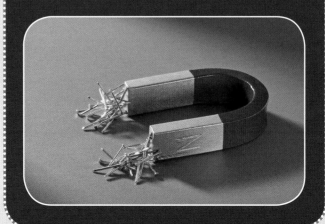

Opposites Attract

Grab two magnets. Hold the north and south poles together. They stick. That's because their forces flow in the same direction. Now try to hold the two north poles together. The magnets push away from each other. Their forces flow in opposite directions.

Friction

Rub your hands together. Can you feel them sliding against each other? You just made friction! Friction is a force. It happens when two surfaces touch each other. Friction can slow down and stop objects.

Smooth surfaces don't have much friction. Wood floors, ice, and glass are easy to slide across. Rough surfaces have more friction. Concrete, carpet, and rubber are hard to slide across.

Our bone joints are covered with cartilage. Cartilage reduces friction in our joints. Too much friction would make it painful to move.

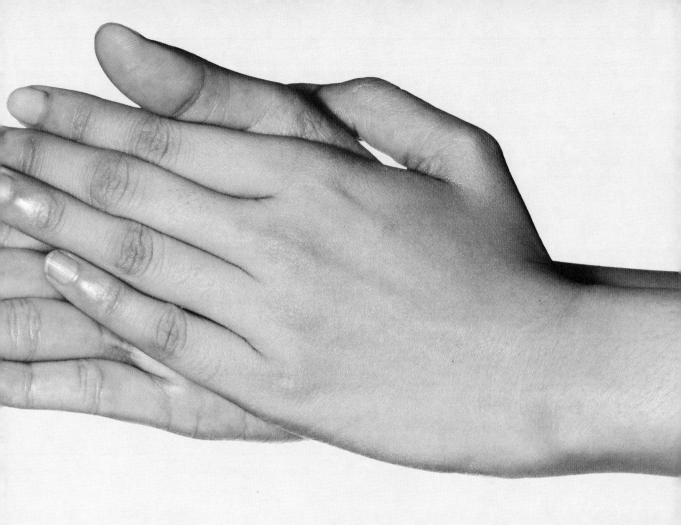

Objects Use Friction

Many objects use friction. Wheels reduce friction. They make it easier to move objects over rough surfaces. Brakes make more friction. They slow down and stop vehicles. A doorstop also creates friction. It sticks to the floor and keeps a door from closing.

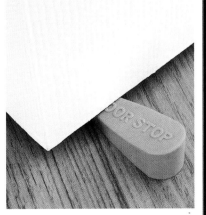

17

Drag

Drag is a type of friction. Drag presses against anything that is moving through air. When air hits an airplane, it makes friction. Drag slows down the plane.

Water has friction. Many sea creatures have smooth bodies. Their shape helps them easily swim through water.

Airplanes have to overcome drag in order to fly. A plane's body must be smooth and thin. A smooth, thin shape passes through air more easily. It makes less drag.

Skydivers use parachutes when they jump from a plane. Parachutes create drag. This slows down the skydivers as they fall to Earth.

Picking Up Speed

An object in motion has speed. Speed is how fast something is moving. You have speed when you walk, run, or swim. A car has speed when your parents drive it down the road. When the car stops, it has no speed.

Sometimes moving objects speed up. They might also change direction. This is called acceleration.

A car that is moving at a constant speed in a straight line has no acceleration.

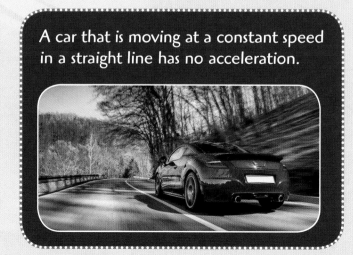

A heavy object has more mass than a light object. It needs a stronger force to push or pull it.

Push an empty box across the floor as hard as you can. It's easy. Next fill the box with books, toys, or even your little brother! Now try to push it with the same amount of force. The full box is not as easy to speed up.

Applying Force

If the same force is applied to each box, the empty box will go farther. It has less mass than the full box. It's easier to push.

force

Slowing Down

Imagine that you're swinging at the park. It's time to go. You dig your feet into the ground. This force stops you from moving. Momentum is how hard it is to stop a moving object. Your body didn't have much momentum. It's easy to stop swinging.

Heavier objects are harder to stop than lighter objects. A race car speeding around a track has a lot of momentum. The race car's brakes must apply a strong force to stop it.

Objects that aren't moving have no momentum.

Balanced and Unbalanced

Forces come in pairs. But not all forces cause motion. Sit on a chair. Your body is pushing down. The chair is pushing up. These forces are balanced. You don't move.

When the forces are unbalanced, there is motion. Raise your arm. Your muscles make your arm go up. At the same time, gravity is pulling your arm down. Your arm is stronger than gravity's pull.

Fish use Newton's Third Law of Motion to swim. Fish push water backward using fins. The water pushes the fins forward with an equal force.

body pushing down

chair pushing up

Predicting Motion

You can use the Laws of Motion to guess how something will move. Imagine you are riding your bike in a straight line. You turn the handlebars to the right. What will happen? The wheel turns the bike to the right.

Now imagine you aren't paying attention. Your bike's front tire hits the curb. What happens? An object in motion needs a force to stop it. The curb stops the bike. But it doesn't stop you. You fly forward over the handlebars. Gravity and the ground stop your motion.

Patterns in motion are all around us. If you look for patterns in motion, they will help you predict future motion.

No great discovery was ever made without a bold guess.

—Isaac Newton

Tools that Cause Motion

You use tools that cause motion every day. Rollerblades let you glide across the ground. A swing sends you soaring through the air. Pedals on your bicycle move the wheels. Hinges on your locker door allow it to swing open and closed.

Glossary

acceleration (ak-sel-uh-RAY-shuhn)—the increasing speed of a moving object

cartilage (KAHR-tuh-lij)—a strong, rubbery tissue that connects bones in people and animals

drag (DRAG)—the force that resists the motion of an object moving through the air

force (FORS)—push or pull

friction (FRIK-shuhn)—a force produced when two objects rub against each other; friction slows down objects

gravity (GRAV-uh-tee)—a force that pulls objects together

mass (MASS)—the amount of material in an object

matter (MAT-ur)—anything that has mass and takes up space

momentum (moh-MEN-tuhm)—a property of a body in motion due to mass and speed

speed (SPEED)—how fast something moves

tide (TIDE)—the rising and falling of ocean water

Critical Thinking Questions

1. What are the Three Laws of Motion? Who discovered them?

2. What is the difference between speed and acceleration?

3. Step outside. What kinds of motion do you see?

Read More

Connors, Kathleen. *Forces and Motion.* A Look at Physical Science. New York: Gareth Stevens Publishing, 2019.

Dunne, Abbie. *Forces.* Physical Science. North Mankato, MN: Capstone Press, 2017.

Sullivan, Laura. *How Do Objects Move?* How Does It Move? Forces and Motion. New York: Cavendish Square Publishing, 2019.

Internet Sites

DK Find Out. Forces and Motion.
https://www.dkfindout.com/us/science/forces-and-motion/

Kids Discover. Force and Motion.
http://www.kidsdiscover.com/spotlight/force-motion-kids/

Physics 4 Kids. Forces of Nature.
http://www.physics4kids.com/files/motion_force.html

Index